Printed in Great Britain
by Amazon

36927260R00061